dabblelab
Drawing Fun with Scooby-Doo!

DRAWING CREEPY CREATURES
with SCOOBY-DOO!

by Steve Korté

illustrated by Scott Jeralds

CAPSTONE PRESS
a capstone imprint

Published by Capstone Press, an imprint of Capstone.
1710 Roe Crest Drive
North Mankato, Minnesota 56003
capstonepub.com

Library of Congress Cataloging-in-Publication Data
Names: Korté, Steven, author. | Jeralds, Scott, illustrator.
Title: Drawing creepy creatures with Scooby-Doo! / by Steve Korté ; illustrated by Scott Jeralds.
Description: North Mankato, Minnesota : Capstone Press, [2022] | Series: Drawing fun with Scooby-
Doo! | Includes bibliographical references. | Audience: Ages 8–11 | Audience: Grades 4–6 | Summary:
"The secrets to drawing Scooby-Doo's creepiest creatures are about to be revealed! With step-by-step
instructions, you'll sketch the Beast of Bottomless Lake, the Creepy Heap from the Deep, the Octopus
Monster, and so much more! Best of all, drawing these classic Scooby characters has never been more
fun and easy!"—Provided by publisher.
Identifiers: LCCN 2021030725 | ISBN 9781663958853 (hardcover)
Subjects: LCSH: Monsters in art—Juvenile literature. | Cartoon characters in art—Juvenile literature. |
Drawing—Technique—Juvenile literature. | Scooby-Doo (Fictitious character)—Juvenile literature.
Classification: LCC NC1764.8.M65 K67 2022 | DDC 743.6—dc23
LC record available at https://lccn.loc.gov/2021030725

Editorial Credits
Christopher Harbo, Editor; Tracy Davies, Designer;
Katy LaVigne, Pre-Media Specialist

Design Elements
Shutterstock: BNP Design Studio, Ori Artiste, sidmay

Printed and bound in the USA.   4608

TABLE OF CONTENTS

LET'S DRAW CREEPY CREATURES WITH SCOOBY-DOO!

It's after midnight in Crystal Cove, and a thick fog is drifting through the nighttime air. Tonight, the five brave members of Mystery Inc. are traveling inside their brightly colored Mystery Machine van. They are patrolling the town's dark streets. Fred Jones is driving. Fellow team members Velma Dinkley and Daphne Blake are sitting near him. And at the back of the van, Shaggy Rogers is sharing a big bag of snacks with his canine pal, Scooby-Doo. The Mystery Inc. gang is on the lookout for more than a dozen frightening monsters and fearsome beasts that have been terrorizing the town.

The brakes of the Mystery Machine squeal as Fred suddenly brings the van to a stop.

"Hang on, gang!" says Fred. "I see our first creepy creature up ahead!"

Scooby-Doo gulps and nervously says, "Ruh-roh!"

Shaggy looks sadly at all the snacks that have fallen onto the floor of the van. "I can still eat these, right?" he asks hopefully.

Over the years, Mystery Inc. has battled a collection of terrifying monsters. Let's see what kind of creepy creatures you can draw!

WHAT YOU'LL NEED

You are about to draw an especially gruesome group of creatures! But you'll need some basic tools to draw these scary monsters. Gather the following supplies before starting your spooky art.

paper

You can get special drawing paper from art supply and hobby stores. But any type of blank, unlined paper will work fine.

pencils

Drawings should always be done in pencil first. Even the pros use them. If you make a mistake, it'll be easy to erase and redo it. Keep plenty of these essential drawing tools on hand.

pencil sharpener

To make clean lines, you need to keep your pencils sharp. Get a good pencil sharpener. You'll use it a lot.

erasers

As you draw, you're sure to make mistakes. Erasers give artists the power to turn back time and undo those mistakes. Get some high-quality rubber or kneaded erasers. They'll last a lot longer than pencil erasers.

black marker pens

When your drawing is ready, trace over the final lines with a black marker pen. The black lines will help make your characters stand out on the page.

colored pens and markers

Ready to finish your masterpiece? Bring your characters to life and give them some color with colored pencils or markers.

The Beast of Bottomless Lake

1

In the Canadian town of Bottomless Lake, an underwater humanoid fish creature has scared away all but three people. It has glowing yellow eyes, dangerous claws, and razor-sharp teeth. Now it's up to the Mystery Inc. gang to slip into scuba suits, hit the water, and capture this slimy monster!

2

3

4

5

Creepy Heap from the Deep

This freaky-looking monster is guaranteed to spoil any beach party! It has one giant eye, green seaweed atop its head, and dangerously sharp, crablike claws. "Watch out for those claws, gang!" calls out Fred as the Mystery Inc. gang gets ready to battle the Creepy Heap from the Deep.

1

dRawing idea
After you draw this creepy creature, add a frightened Scooby-Doo to your picture.

8

2

3

4

5

Creature from the Chem Lab

1

A claw-handed monster is scaring the students at Hillside High. Cheerleaders run from the gym screaming in fear when the creature arrives. It's up to Mystery Inc. to find out if the monster was created in the school's chemistry lab. And it's up to you to draw this beast.

2

3

4

5

Greek Minotaur

In old tales of Greek mythology, the Minotaur was a fierce monster with the head of a bull and the body of a man. But Minotaurs don't really exist, right? "Zoinks!" yells Shaggy when he and Scooby meet a raging beast on a Greek island.

1

dRawing idea

Add a scared Shaggy to your drawing of the Minotaur. Maybe show Shaggy dropping his bag of snacks when he sees the monster.

2

3

4

5

Gator Ghoul

A mysterious alligator creature known as the Gator Ghoul is haunting the Hokefenokee Swamp and scaring away customers at Ma and Pa Skillet's restaurant. Can Scooby-Doo and his cousin Scooby-Dum cook up a way to save the business?

1

dRawing idea
Show Scooby-Doo and his cousin Scooby-Dum chasing the Gator Ghoul.

2

3

4

5

Jaguaro

Deep within a Brazilian jungle lurks a massive beast with the body of a brown gorilla and the head of a black saber-tooth tiger. It's the ferocious monster known as the Jaguaro. When the Mystery Inc. gang shows up in that same jungle, Scooby and Shaggy just might end up as snacks for this creepy creature!

1

dRawing idea

Add a jungle background to your drawing. You can include lots of trees and maybe some colorful tropical birds, such as parrots.

2

3

4

5

Ape Man

Lights! Camera! Action! Is that an actor or a dangerous ape causing trouble on the movie set for *The Ape Man of Forbidden Mountain*? It's up to Mystery Inc. to answer that question before the scary creature harms anyone.

1

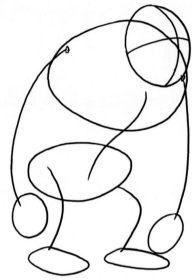

dRawing idea

The next time you draw the Ape Man, show him on a movie set next to bright lights, a movie camera, and a film director.

2

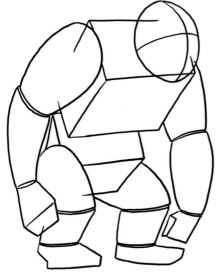

3

4

5

Demon Shark

1

Maybe it wasn't the smartest thing Scooby-Doo ever did when he decided to eat an egg, cheese, and hot dog sandwich while out water-skiing. That's just the kind of thing that might attract a hungry half-man and half-fish creature known as the Demon Shark!

dRawing idea

The next time you draw the Demon Shark, show him leaping out of the ocean's waves.

2

3

4

5

Abominable Snowman

The Abominable Snowman is a giant creature that lives high atop a snow-capped mountain. He is covered from head to toe in white fur, and he has a fierce temper. When Scooby makes the mistake of skiing too close to this dangerous monster, it's up to the rest of the gang to rescue him.

1

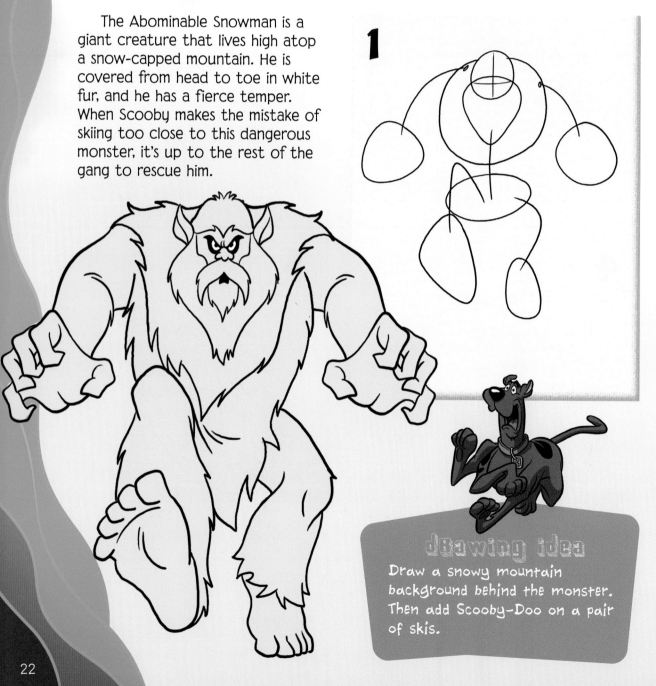

drawing idea

Draw a snowy mountain background behind the monster. Then add Scooby-Doo on a pair of skis.

2

3

4

5

Octopus Monster

What has wiggling tentacles, a mouth full of sharp teeth, and a dangerous appetite? It's the Octopus Monster! This slimy creature is guarding a sunken pirate ship filled with treasures—and it will gobble up anyone that gets too close!

1

Mantis

1

"Jeepers!' says Daphne while visiting Vulture's Claw Botanical Garden. She has just encountered a terrifying, seven-foot-tall bug known as Mantis. Where did this giant praying mantis come from? Was it the result of an experiment gone wrong? And how will Daphne and the gang escape from it?

2

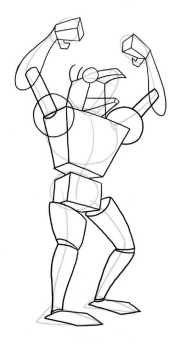

3

4

5

Unmasking the Gator Ghoul

Ruh-roh! The Mystery Inc. gang has cornered the Gator Ghoul in the Hokefenokee Swamp. The monster hisses and flashes its dangerously sharp teeth. "Hang on, gang!" says Fred as he bravely grabs the Gator Ghoul's head and removes its mask. The monster is really an angry restaurant employee named Alice Dovely. Mystery Inc. has saved the day!

1

2

3

4

5

MORE DRAWING FUN!

Bird, Benjamin. *Animal Doodles with Scooby-Doo!* North Mankato, MN: Capstone Press, 2017.

Harbo, Christopher. *10-Minute Drawing Projects.* North Mankato, MN: Capstone Press, 2020.

Sautter, Aaron. *How to Draw Superman and His Friends and Foes.* North Mankato, MN: Capstone Press, 2015.

MORE SCOOBY-DOO FUN!

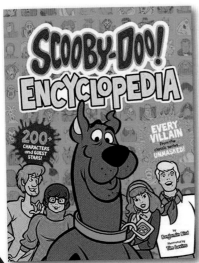

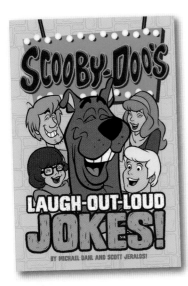

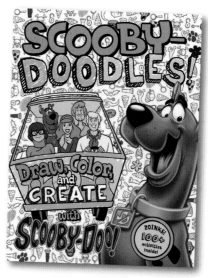